By the Stroke of My Hand

*Poems by a Stroke Survivor
and Natural Wordsmith*

Thomas Clelland

ISBN: Softcover   978-1-6641-1616-0
               eBook   978-1-6641-1615-3

All illustrations have been created by Thomas Clelland.

Print information available on the last page.

Rev. date: 03/15/2022

To order additional copies of this book, contact:
Xlibris
UK TFN: 0800 0148620 (Toll Free inside the UK)
UK Local: (02) 0369 56328 (+44 20 3695 6328 from outside the UK)
www.Xlibrispublishing.co.uk
Orders@Xlibrispublishing.co.uk
819206

Contents

I have dedicated my book to all stroke
survivors and their carers.

Acknowledgement

I would like to acknowledge Susan O Evans, a North London Hospice Compassionate Neighbour. She saw the vision of creating a book of my poems and without her support you would not be reading this book right now.

True Patience

Been in hospital many times and they say that we are the patients
But the real meaning of the patients
Are the gallant band who have the patience day and night within and without a fuss
Always smiling and having the patience to look after those who need it most
Sometimes without thanks sometimes with thanks
But the real meaning of patients are the patient people who look after us day and night
Without them we would be in a terrible plight
So thank you for all of you doctors nurses
And all the others who have the patience to see it through
So the real meaning of patients are the ones
Who always have the patience with us without a fuss

Introduction by Thomas Clelland

Well the nature poem I was walking through the park one day and I noticed all the things that people don't notice and I talked to myself - invisible leaves falling from the trees calculated colours on the breeze. It's like nature is everywhere but they say money don't grow on trees so nobody see the beauty in nature. I see how many people walk through the park. Do they notice how fantastic they are all on their own? I guess that's what it's about really. People just take for granted what they've got in front of them and that's why I wrote the poem invisible leaves falling from the trees calculating colours on the breeze. I write a lot of poetry like this completely off the cuff in 5-minutes. I can take any subject and turn it into a poem - that's my gift. I notice these things you see such as trees. The very strong branches could snap a man in two but when the wind blows instead of resisting the trees go with the branches; always sway with the wind and I thought if people could be like that it would be better for them instead of always trying to resist. You see if the branch resists the wind on the tree the branch would snap and fall off but they don't resist they just go with the wind. Just a thought, a very interesting thought.

I am hoping my poems will help stroke survivors express what they are feeling and experiencing with their carer's in a more expressive way.

I can be contacted by email at crcrosst@gmail.com.

The Stroke

Dizzy falling into space
Where death and life have no trace
Twirling, whirring round and round
In the air, can't hear a sound.

The ground has gone.
Tell me where the ground has gone.

You reach for something, a sudden shock.
Your mind begins to run amok.
Your brain's gone wild; the circuits don't respond.

The ground has gone.
Tell me where the ground has gone?

You put your feet upon the ground.
But no ground can be found,
Except a dizzy, whirring sound.

You reach for something to support,
And find yourself finally on the ground.
This time you can't get up,
You lay there on the ground.

But still gravity flees from your brain,
You find once more where you remain, can't move.
Your legs can't walk, your arms are numb,
Your speech is slurred.

So no one knows what's going on,
Except you and your Stroke.

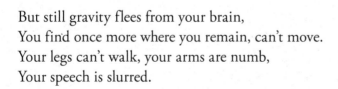

Strange Land

I fell upon the ground and find myself in this strange land.
A strange land I can't recall.
I can't remember when I fell or if I fell at all.
This strange land is not green and pleasant.

It is rugged, sharp, and undecidable.
I can't find it where I want to be.
I look around what I want to see,
There is nothing there for me.

This strange land, I have to find it again.
With all the worries, doubt, and pain,
This strange land comes back again to my mind.
I flounder in this land.

So many hold out there hand,
But they can't understand.
It is a strange land, strange customs,
Strange world, strange thoughts.

People say a new beginning,
But I think not as I ought.
I tell myself in this strange land,
It is like there has to be a plan.

But I can't plan in this strange land,
And I don't understand this strange land.
There is a maze around me,
A fog, a fog distance that I can't understand.

I feel I could run and run and run and run,
Never going anywhere.
I feel I should sit down, but where would I go sitting down?
The feelings that I have I can't move.

But I can't take them lightly in this strange land; that's the truth.
It is a land of nowhere.
Thoughts I have are dim and distant.
The land I was before was easier to explore.

I found this place, I found that place,
Just as I found countless times before.
The land I'm in now,
Is a land I don't know.

I grope around; I find this wherever to go,
The shadows follow me.
I don't want the memories of the past,
But in the strange land the shadows seem to last.

Distressing fantasies follow me around.
I wouldn't say it was pleasant.
I'd say it was like someone took me up a mountain
With ragged rocks and steep hills and left me there.

I was trying to figure out how to get down,
I'm in a boat, and I find out I had no oars.
All I can do is drift with no oars,
And rely on some other force to find another course.

The Little Man

The little man inside my head is acting like a child.
He's turning all the dials around, and all the wires he's changed.
And all I feel right now Is confusion in my brain.
I'd like to ask that little man to put the plugs right back.
He knows where they all are; can't he put them back?
I tried to change it by myself, but strange enough, it seems
The little man has altered my mind, thoughts, and my dreams.
The little man inside my head has changed the wires around.
I try to find a thought I had before, but now it can't be found.
I'm looking to the future, but the future seems so bleak.
That little man inside my head tries to make me speak.
Before I used to go and have no feelings.
That changed me, controlled me.
Now I find out he's turned my plugs around.
This circuit isn't the same; no more the same can be found.
It's like that little man inside my head, he's changed the plugs around.
He's acting like a little child and turned me upside down.
I don't understand what's going on.
It seems to me too strong that I'm fighting, but I cannot say.
Other would say to me depression is the key,
But I still cannot unlock the door to my reality.
But the wires seem to have been changed, but how do I get them back?
Maybe the little man, in too much of a hurry, made one of the little plugs crack.
And now I feel my head is whirling, going round and round.
I am looking for the little man but the little man cannot be found.

Invisible Leaves

Invisible leaves fall from the trees.
Wintertime is near.
Calculated colours on the breeze.

Can it be that sincere?
A blanket of gold upon the ground
More valuable than can be
Found to astound the educated.

Nature always stays in time,
rehearsing all the day and night
The song of birds, the silent words still spoken by the flowers.
Nature screams at us,
Come see the real reality
Of what it is to be not metal, plastic fantasies of man.

But somewhere in a perfect plan it tells us,
"Beware. See the flowers, trees, and nature's ease,
Revealing, expounding, exploding."
Please don't pass us by,
Lest one day soon there will be no room to plant or reap or sow.

Invisible leaves fall from the trees,
Calculated colours on the breeze.
Let's hope they never disappear.
Because of man's hunger to progress whatever,
Might be the price.

The Messenger

The messenger

Unexpectedly he came, the messenger who had no name.
Some say he was a priest, others a fool.
But those who had nothing to say were the ones to benefit most of all.
From his eyes there was no earth, neither was their sun.
But one of peace as of the birds in flight,
Minnowed by the night.

The crowd just gathered round, and around, but nothing from the
stranger came.
No one heard a sound.

Then suddenly the stranger spoke, and all the crowd began to shake.
He said that words are such a precious gift to wake from the deep sleep.
You have the gift, but like a ruby thrown in the gutter,
Mutter, mutter, mutter.

Realise when words are used with depths of love can tear the chains away,
Can make your gift to shine so bright, whereas in the gutter it lay.
And as he spoke, the crowd seemed to mutter more and more,

Suddenly, without warning, he disappeared behind the door.
And high above, a pure white cloud mauve smoke was seen so clear,
And yet the crowd still talked so loud.

Unexpectedly, he came the messenger who had no name,
And as he came, and so he disappeared just the same.
But the crowd still seem to throw their rubies in the gutter,
Just to be washed away by the waterslide or maybe man's indifference.

Blind Ambition

Waves, waves upon the brain, the sane man stays away,
The foolish step right in and claims the prize.
Blind ambition
What tries and lies and dies, and yet again revives?
Blind ambition
Loses itself in itself deep to sleep, but is never sad to weep for lost treasure.
Blind ambition
Man's transition is from division of his senses to awaken his defenses,
and always there's a voice, it's chanting,
"Blind ambition."
A weak becomes a strong from a thong of impotence, and laughs at
pain and trouble just to double the last applause.
Is the crown worth so much?
Blind ambition says it is
"Ten times ten times, and then
again no more."
Ambition is a proud teacher, a
vain preacher
Be careful least you all fall into its
timeless trap.
Waves, waves upon the brain,
The sane man stays away,
The foolish steps right.
And claims the prize.

The Mirror

Sometimes I get the feeling that I'm not here at all,
That every face is a reflection in a huge almighty pool.
And when the water is disturbed by hand or stick or stone,
Then all the faces disappear, and I am left alone.

I see all the faces reflected in the pool.
Some look vacant, some obscene.
Some like their eyes are on fire, and
Some like love has never been.

But who are the ones that are reflections, and
Who are the ones who that are real;
And who, after all, is a mirror
To what everyone else wants to feel.

It's easy to be lost in nothing.
You just fall till you can't fall no more.
You just break the reflections,
That make up the water,
And the mirror is smashed on the floor.

So one day I'll empty the water.
I'll shatter the mirror, you'll see,
Then there'll be no more reflections.
Just a simple reality. Me.

The mirror

Writer's block

The .wall .

If all the poets run out of rhyme and the singers lost all their songs
Think what a strange world it would be if the world would see nothing wrong.
But where would imagination go and the things that the world cannot see
All of the things that the world doesn't hear would somehow cease to be
And all of the things that make people dream
Seeing beyond the dark
Into man's world of eternity somebody lights a spark.

A poet writes reunites and fills the air with prose and proverbs
A singer moves the sky the soul sound and a message that erupts into 1000 melodies
Inspiration where does it come from the night the day a 1000 memories at play
The world would say one less singer that's ok
Exist for the soul
The breathing changing harmony soul

I used to make songs of everything
If I saw a field it would turn into a war

I only had to think something from it came a song and spiraling into words and words
I never knew where it came from when the words would go not knowing where it is
I knew bathing in a brand new day
But no one else had heard

I could stand around and watch the morning
There be another room filled with Starlight and love and dreams
A dance would come from Melody and take me from this place
I see angels in the garden I was just a child a long time ago
When I was undecided
But now I see the moon it's the moon it's the moon
And the river is the river what's all the fuss about

When I look at the wall all see is my head
When I look in my head all I see is a wall
When I stare at the wall all I see is my head
I have ceased to remain contemplated instead
But there's nothing there where once there was a waterfall
A river and a tree now there is a problem and the problem is me
I cannot see beyond the wall someone could break it down
But then what's behind The Wall
I'm sure it's not safe or sound.

So I'll put up with the wall until it disappears
And maybe with it's going also will go my fears
I'm stretching pushing pulling pleading just to lose the wall
And maybe then the miracle of songs will return again
But I'm not sure for now
Anyway, the wall is all I see now pretty words for careful rhymes
I know dreaming is eccentricity but walls on walls that block the way to my eternity.

13

Clouds

Clouds they drift and flow
And fade and grow across the never-ending sky
No one knows changing clouds they fade away another day
Another tapestry is a pattern that is born from nowhere

Clouds a new formation for concentration understand sometimes grey
sometimes white
They bring the message to us with their colours in the sky
And tell us how the day will be as we are walking by
Clouds they say if clouds are grey life could be dismay
They say if clouds are white must be a good day to let the sun spread
It's light through all of the dismay

Clouds they reach up to the sky
And first of all they taught us how to fly
You look at birds they rise so high
Without the clouds where would they be?
A measuring stick for infinity
And finally divinity we can't see

Clouds form their patterns for us everyday
But do we understand they're trying to say
Hey let's look again into the skies
And see the clouds with different kinds of eyes

Without Love

Without Love there is no meaning life has no meaning
It is just the time of day
That goes on and on and on is on its way
Without love it makes it special to have love
Because it seems to come from somewhere beyond
When you love life has a meaning it takes you through the ceiling
Gives you a feeling that you cannot understand
And when you feel that way no one can explain it
Because it's love

Without Love there is no meaning
Ok no night-time in flight just never ever to be here
Without Love there is without a lover and a friend
No life companionship togetherness just a lonely feeling
Things going on time it's gone and times all the same again
Without Love there is a loneliness
No-one can understand because it's there nothings planned
But it's an end this day and end this time of living
Without the one to love

Love is a special time and without it you have no mind
To see something that's fine because love is something you cannot define
You cannot define love when it happens
You don't know why
When it is you don't even try to understand
You look for something to plan
But love cannot be planned it's another world when it happens
You'll know

The Fool

The fool met the fool on the highway,
Saying, "I know this is foolish.
Can you tell me the direction on this byway?"

The fool said, "I am a fool.
Why are you asking me at all?
Should I know the answer to this foolish question?"

"That's why I'm asking.
What we both seem to do,
Is answer foolish questions all the time.

But this is not a foolish question,
And the answer is quite plain.
Stay away from foolish fools,
And keep your distance from me.

Go back to the sane and normal.
And you will find direction,
In a much more foolish way.
Because the fool only finds the answer,
When the wise man stays away."

I am a silent face

I am a silent face part of the crowd quite soft sometimes loud
The friends that I have made face I do not speak
I do not need fame when I join the friends and we make beautiful sounds
There's nothing quite like it from anywhere around

I am a silent face
Nothing can replace even if it's something else
I am a silent face
I am the silent place in the choir
I make up the masses but I make up the sound
Which has many many shapes and sizes

I am the silent face
In the orchestra I play at least if my instrument wasn't there
Where would you be In this mayhem
Because they would be part of the place that I play
When I say that place that's where I am

As I can to make myself to understand and others too
I don't mind being part of something do you
It might mean you're never recognised
But you are part of the cog compartment of the wheel
And part of the thing that keeps everything going

In this silent place at the silent face whenever I play play
Whatever it sounds it could be the big drum or the castanet
Or the tambourine but all these things fit into the one big performance
and scheme

I'm looking for
Mr Right

I'm looking for Mr Right she said as she carefully tossed her head
I know exactly who he is
He is soft powerful gentle considerate my shining armour Knight Mr Right
He won't do a thing wrong
He will always sing my song to travel on together with no problems at
all the perfect Shangri-La of all my dreams come true
I'm looking for Mr Right she said
The man beside her sadly
Shook his head and said you'll never know

I'm looking for Mrs Right he said
Someone in my thoughts and dreams
She's perfect quite unique beautiful voice lovely eyes nice to look at
everything I want I need
And take heed here's the only one I have to find Mrs right
Otherwise I stay alone and dream all on my own
Mrs Right is coming very soon
I can't consider anyone else she has to be perfect
In every aspect I won't settle for anyone else
Mrs Right is in My dreams thoughts where are you Mrs right

So sad that these two characters don't exist
They are sad to say always missed by everyone who are looking for the
perfect one
Whilst others in front of you you pass by
So time is short don't waste it with the one that you can't see
Face reality with the ones you can
Before they're all gone.
And it's too late to fulfill your Destiny

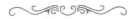

Do you see my love

Do you see my love
You see my puzzled look of apprehension for humanities course
See the thoughts that I have
Simple living, and trying
But do you see my love

You see the day to day expression of my eyes in slumber
Or in sleep
You see my crazy face that clowning smile
When people need to stay a while
And feel a comfort

You see the heavy man or woman discussing topics
Of relevant change
But do you see my love
You see the darkness, and the anger of the person
I could become or want to run away from
To feel the kindness that is given
When for some unknown reason tears fall to the ground
But do you see my love

You see the pity that I have in my eyes and can't disguise
For people who cannot break the barrier of emotion
Losing themselves to an expression of indifferences
But do you see my love

You show me what it's like to be old and young at the same time
A child and a man girl and a woman
You see the fears that come for every individual faced with reality or
imagination
But do you see my love

You see the task to understand
The striving to become
But do you see my love

If you don't see my love then I can't see at all

There's a window

There's a window in the sky,
And I'm going to fly.
I can see it very clear.
I'll rise up from the ground
And upwards I shall go until I reach that window
In the sky.
Then a door will open,
And I'll just say goodbye.

Providing no one gets in my way.
This is the illusion; the reality is forever.
If it was that simple
And I could go right now,
And I can see that window,
In the sky.

I'd rise up this moment
Until I reached that window.
Then I'd walk in through that window,
And say goodbye.

There's a window in the sky,
You can't see it with your eyes.
But it's there, deep in your spirit.
We'll all fly.

I should have spent more time

I should have spent more time with you when I was there.
Never mind.
Moments are so valuable, and they never come again
Whether shared with your lover or shared with a friend.

The ceasing time of time rolls on into the day,
And passes very quickly.
One moment you're at play.
And next moment you are standing at the crossroads,

And as you contemplate the time,
Of when you shared your dream.
The morning becomes the evening,
And the shadows start to scream.

Hey, where have you been?
Didn't you notice the potentate of time?
Just disappearing through the haze,
And slowly in your mind.

The moments are so valuable,
And value counts so few.
Your loved ones and your dearest,
Make sure you share the best moments with them too.

My dog ran away with my breakfast

My dog ran away with my breakfast
The postman delivered the wrong parcel
The bus driver passed out on the way to work
A sea gull came in and stole my grapes of the table
I lost my keys and had to climb in through a 3 storey window
And a neighbour reported me to the Police
I spent last night under a suspect in a cell
On top of that I found a fish in my bath
l was grateful because the cat got the fish
I backed out of the gate and hit a fender
It was a sunday so I couldn't find anyone
I came home and my flat had been stripped
My girlfriend had emptied out my flat and
Bank account and found a newer version
I decided to wash the car closed the window
With my keys in the ignition trying to charge the battery
Just then the dog came back with my breakfast
At least I got my breakfast

People are like drops of rain

People are like drops of rain
They come and go and they're gone again like drops of rain
Passing through you once again expressing to you their role
Who they are, and then they're gone like a blazing fire in the night out of control

People are like drops of rain they come and go
When dark clouds appear clouds full of water needs to disperse on everyone around
Same as the people who meet each other they say hello
And then the next they cannot be found

Like drops of rain they come into your life, and like drops of rain they go
You cannot hold onto them you know
It's not easy to hold onto drops of rain
As it's not easy to hold onto people who pass your way
Though like rain on your face then it's gone
When the sun comes out to replace the dark clouds in the sky

Some people come not like drops of rain
But like sunshine and a smile these
People are the ones who stay for a while
Like drops of rain on a sunny day you cannot tell
When it goes away when it comes again
The same as people when they come
And they go and they don't remain

People are like drops of rain
They pass through your life and they never remain

But the ones who do remain
When the drops of rain just disappear
Cause much more sunshine to appear.

In your life you feel much stronger because much longer is the time
this day will bring
Most of the time like drops of rain people have to go their way
And as we do not understand the rain it's the same with people again
and again
We don't know where the rain comes from it's like a cloud and then
it's gone

Sometimes when you meet someone they're just like that
Then as mysteriously as they come they're gone out of your life
So my friend
Accept the dark clouds and accept the sunshine too
And remember people are like drops of rain
Will never take you to a place you need to go
Because like drops of rain they're gone you know

And if you need to hold onto someone in your life
Hold on to the sunshine and the clouds will disappear
And very soon those who care for you the most will always be very near

Consequence and circumstance

Consequence and circumstance
We're talking to each other what was going on
They began to speak to each other
Consequences for staying in the choices that we have made
I am consequences I've guided you from many scenes
And look where it's got you now

Circumstance was saying
What can I say to you
Maybe you should have considered things you had to do
How dare you talk to me said consequence so loud
Look where you are today because of me

Consequences blurted out yes look where I am today because of you
Suddenly they met traveler Reality his name
He said I take it you have an argument
Circumstance said it almost comes out the same
This has to replace the replace the consequence

So much you could have replaced on your journey through life
But you didn't consider the circumstances what were they like
Then suddenly reality spoke said this is where you are right now
More of the twists and turns you had
And all the sadness happiness and all the things that made you glad
And all the time you changed the consequences

This is where you are right now
If you do not consider that time you got you will lose it again
Somehow the precious minutes going by the seconds knew
Just grab the day and grab the time
Well my friend it's up to you

A place called youth

A place called youth
What was that place called youth?
A place of Truth or was it just a lie?
Where you all realise and why
Where we didn't care about the time
Because the time was never precious but wasted on the moment

What was that place called youth a place of Truth
Where we spent half nights raising the roof
Listening to music so loud it could burst our ears
And tears were another love affair
What is worse we never noticed anyone around us who we found only
those amusing of our choosing

Was that place called youth a place of Truth
In the past it couldn't last we had to move along
And sing another song and how long could it be if we were wrong or right
We never considered that as we stayed up half the night
To raise the roof and listen to the songs of youth

Was that place called youth a distant past
Was that the only one and now at last is it good to see that yesterday
was better than today
Memories that you have are they better than the days we have right
now or the days we know somehow
How to change our lives for the better or for the worst

Was that place called youth a place of Truth
The only place to believe that things could change and as I sit here
now I tried to rearrange my thoughts I'll always keep believing when
I'm leaving that yesterday

Today something warm making me Believe
That you've is always best but then experience
The rest if you never will move along
How can you experience what is right or wrong and learn much more
always moving on into the future.

Illusion and Confusion

If your in confusion can you see through the illusion
Man was walking down the road met a fellow traveler he said you look
like an unraveler
Maybe you are maybe your not but what you remember you might
have forgot
The traveler replied with a wink in his eye
What is it trouble is you my friend
Maybe I can show you the world you don't know and a time that
doesn't find any end

The man he just turned
And said to the traveler this is what troubles me today
If you're in the confusion how do you solve the illusion
Or end it to find a solution the solution my friends
I can understand if you're in the confusion how do you end the illusion
delusion
Is in the confusion and the confusion is in conclusion

If you live in confusion how do you find and end the illusion
It's so strange what I have to say
Because I cannot deal with what I have today
I have such a confusion and I've been fed an illusion which I cannot
understand anyway

If you live in the confusion
All around me I see the confusion in the people's faces that I meet
And they're fed the illusion and so they cannot find anything complete
And when they're looking for the confusion in the illusion that's the
only thing they can feel
And finally I'd like to know why when your in the confusion nothing
is real

The traveler he turned and with his heart burnt an answer
Much more than before he could feel he said
All is illusion the sky the trees the sea they are only
A solution if someone can see that they're real

If you're in the illusion how can you solve the confusion
Because the confusion cannot solve the illusion therefore there is no solution
So I would advise looking at you with my eyes
Do not try to solve the illusion accept the illusion
Get rid of the confusion and then you will find the final solution

Goodbye he said the man there's another road I must take
I can only tell you one thing you haven't solved the problem
There are more decisions I have to make but thank you for the advice
I better think twice before I stay in the confusion and try to solve the illusion
Finally someday come what may I might come to the final conclusion
A parody for today

Does reality
cause dreams

We spend half time in bed he said and then his friend shook his head
have another drink and let me think

Does reality cause dreams or does dreams cause reality?

Interesting I see where you're going when you lose this world
You go somewhere else not awake and not asleep
You're in another world where creeps in the dream and a nothing of it
seems real

Do dreams cause reality or does reality cause dreams?

Our dreams are fleeting pictures of some reality the subconscious in
your fantasy
I wonder as I'm speaking maybe some people live in dreams the whole
world is a dream
And reality is a passing phase you close your eyes and drift off to
another place called time

Do dreams cause reality or does reality cause dreams?

When you sleep where do you go you disappear in dreams you know
You dream unconsciously not knowing what you dream when it
becomes reality
Sometimes you wake up and you scream
The reality is far too much sometimes you feel yourself becoming the
reality
And you have to pinch yourself to realise you are still in touch
If you just keep on going through this dreamy world
Some people say dreams are your reality

Are dreams caused by reality or is reality caused by dreams?

It seems that some people keep on dreaming and one day their dreams
come true
They can be wide awake and dream of things they need to do
There are all sorts of dreams my friend are you wide awake
Or gone to take another journey into the reality of dreams

Reality is only a word quite absurd so who knows are we dreaming or
in reality
Do we really know reality
Some people live in the reality of dreams and never leave them
Some people dream all the time sometimes you're wide awake and you
dream for things to come true
And they say if you dream enough they do
What I wonder to myself

Do dreams cause reality or does reality cause dreams?

It seems there's all sorts of dreams and my question is to you
Whatever you might do
Do dreams cause reality or does reality cause dreams
Goodnight said his friend as he walked off down the road
If its so this is too much for me and I cannot bear this load
But if you feel that's alright and it's shed a tiny bit of light
Then carry on receiving what you do
That's what you have is something that's unique and new
To understand dreams understand reality nobody really has a clue.

Did you lose something on the way?

Did you lose something on the way
There was a time when you were happy and gay
Then you realised you couldn't be that way then you began to not
smile at all
People didn't treat you like a fool

Did you lose something on the way?
It was so long ago you cannot say as a child you trusted everyone
Who came your way trusting everything they said
Never shook your head as if to say hey it's not the truth

Did you lose something on the way?
Something my friend that you cannot replay and it won't come again
So accept it my friends and what did you gain a heart that hard
A mind unfeeling speaking words so harsh and had no meaning

Did you lose something on the way?
From a child it was so innocent
Now you have to be untrusting regretful suspicious
All around don't even trust the words that people say
Unless they can prove something profound

Did you lose something on the way?
Is what you replaced it with something better
Although you lost something and always wanted something more
Now you found something that shackled your heart and soul
Can you shake off the hardness of the years that took you to regret
And to tears and to resentment

Can you shake off what you have become
Trying to find the child once again
You were but if you did could you survive and stay alive soft again
And you wouldn't want that would you?

You need the armour that you hold to combat all the things to you
need to protect
And the things you have to decipher trusting is too strong
Where do you belong in the child or in the one you have become
My friend you can choose which one

What is it all about?

What is it all about?
Was it about something that I tried for?
Something that I use to be satisfied
Look around you brother
What was it all about?

You used to run and used to fly just to swim and cry out now
Were you looking at the flowers and the
sky and wondering if they know
What's it all about?
I wonder said the person who told himself he didn't understand
I reckon it was about something
But most of us keep trying to find out about it all
Some of us don't even try at all

But what was it all about?
Was it something that I tried
Something that needed to be satisfied?
Could I be satisfied with what I wanted to be
Would I have a reached that goal
Maybe I never would maybe I will never find myself
and then I look around me and I wonder
The afternoon is very quiet
Just like a silent night

What was it about you was it about me was it something to be free
What was it about anything at all was it something nice to see
What was it about at all was it something that I needed to find out
Said the man who drew his last breath and said I still don't know

I had a dream
of Charlie

I had a dream of Charlie
Who stood beside my bed
I said this bed is sacred
It's where I lay my head
He said I'm an angel
I watch you when you sleep
I said it's a good job I don't wake up
And have a little peep

I had a dream of Charlie
Funny name for an angel
But whose to tell
You know full well
Time had not consumed

The angel said I'm watching still
I hope you don't mind
They call us guardian angels
We've been here a long time with mankind

I had a dream of Charlie
I know full well right now
I'm not sure what is real
And what I should just tell
Maybe I'll carry on sleeping
What is reality anyway
Just a load of mixed up genes so they say

I'm thankful for Charlie
I know that when I lay my head
The guardian angel
While I'm dreaming will
Stay beside my bed

Don't fall in love with the Barmaid

Don't fall in love with the barmaid
She says darling to every guy
Never fall in love with the barmaid she is there to catch your eye

If you think she means what she's saying
She's a barmaid didn't you know
She's there to pour the beer and watch the money flow

I don't want to disillusion you mate
But she does this to every guy
She's there to earn her wages and a few tips on the sly

Don't fall in love with the barmaid
She smiles as well you see
Because you see with her trade friendship is the key

Don't get too close to the barmaid
There's danger in her eyes
Maybe there's some fella waiting you'd better just think twice

So when you look at the barmaid remember what I've said
Don't get carried away
Don't let it go to your head

But thank the little darlings
For being so warm and nice
But before you fall in love with the barmaid
My friend watch out think twice

Death walks among Us

Death walks among Us
And tells us we are friends
This is the beginning and not the end
Sometimes we plot and plan and do not understand
The ways of time we are
How many days and nights
We've wasted doing things that's never lasted

Death walks among us and tells us we are friends
This is the beginning but not the end
Life is like the blink of an eye so quick so fast
Nothing to rely why do we waste so many days and nights
Being respectable and right not stepping out of line
Because that would not be the thing to do
We do not see it's easy to make mistakes
The things we always knew and wasted
Years and days and nights things we love against our time

Death walks among us and tell us we are friends
This is the beginning and not the end
So my friend let me say don't waste your time on trivial things today
The blinking of an eye goes by so you find you can't rely
One moment you're a little boy
Holding mummy's hands next your standing next to someone
And making wedding plans
And your children's children call you grandad and your bones getting tired
And you wonder where the days went to

One moment your a little girl
Playing with your dolls the next step season all your clothes
The players on the grass

The next you stand up one day
It's always just gone and passed the wedding vows were easy
Oh what a grand affair
But that was long ago and you're sitting in your chair
Wondering where it all went in the blink of an eye don't waste it my friend

It's gone so fast you know the day are like the moment and the moments seem to go
Where did it go
Death walks among us and tells us we are friends
But this is the beginning and not the end

An alien

An alien from so and so
I say hello to people they say hello to me
What if they are aliens in disguise
I cannot tell them as they talk
I cannot see them as they walk
What if they are aliens in disguise?

You know that would explain lot of things the stranger in the bar
You say hello he says hello you turn around he's gone you know
What if half the world were not people at all
That would explain a lot of things the
Alienist to each other
The inability to love your brother
Pretense is a matter of colour or race

I guess the only time you know it's if you love someone
And go to bed have some fun
Surely this person in your bed who's snuggles up
Against your head must be from this planet you said

Do you really know what if
Everyone you know
Is one of these or one of those
Did you ever examine their right foot
Or maybe they got a hidden nose
I'm telling you really there's no way you can know
Whether they're from planet Earth
Or an alien from so and so

Next time you talk to someone and they leave as you say hello
They might be disguising
That you're realising they're an alien from
So and so

Look at every sunset

Look at every sunset.
And look at every sunrise.
Don't let the day go,
Not knowing if you lived it.

If you have to give yourself,
Look at every sunrise.
Don't let the day go,
Not knowing if you lived it.

If you give to yourself everything you could give,
And every second of the experience you lived.
Look at every sunset,
Look at every sunrise.

Don't forget the moment that you live,
Is the moment you can give to yourself.
Don't waste in haste the time you spend.
Observe a tree, and watch when winds come
How those mighty branches yield themselves
To a stronger force, to branches that can crack a skull,
Just bend to the wind.

Look at every sunset.
Look at every sunrise.
Now has gone wasting time,
Days and months and minutes.
Pass on their way; another,
One has gone today.

Take care of your sunsets.
Live each day with vigour and with power.
And each hour
Thanking God for each sunrise that you see.
Do not waste the speed of time which,
Rolls on and on and on.

Soon it will be gone,
Everything you could give.
And every second of the experience to live.
Look at every sunrise.
Look at every sunset.

Eyes that dance

Eyes that entrance and eyes that just dance
And eyes that just say stay awhile
Eyes with a smile, eyes with a frown
Eyes say I'm glad you're around
Eyes that entrance, eyes that just dance
Eyes that can pull you into another dimension
Leaving you lost in a time of dissention
You pay the cost for the eyes
The eyes of a child, bright-eyed and wild
The eyes of an adult, dark and defiled
Someone has taken the trust
The eyes show it, all the sadness, the grief, the time for a time when
there was no one to believe
The eyes show the lovers and haters on the way
It's all in the eyes; look closely my friend, you'll see all the truth in the eyes
Be careful with your eyes, and don't use disguise to entrance or deceive
One day someone will look in your eyes and say, "I accept, I believe."

There's a tiger

Time is a tiger that roars every day,
Looking for someone's existence to pay.
Time has no passion, no remorse, no regret,
Time travels on with no changing yet.
And while we are musing on time's timeless trap,
It's moving beneath us as we sit and yap.
But time is a tiger; it will waste you too,
Unless you can fill each day with time's time to do.
Don't let it go by or waste it; time flies, and while we are,
Speaking, another idea dies.
But pick up today with all speed and array,
And steal it and live it and don't let it steal you away.

Dust Is the Key

When everything I know turns into dust
And everything we see loses its trust
Then all our life
Is what we can't see
I believe that's the only reality

I look at the dreams and aspirations
Of people I knew
All based on what you are and what you can do
But that's not reality

Dust is the key
Don't trust in a pretty face
Or enticing words
They all just fade aswel as age; a boyish look
A girly smile don't last
They've been there awhile

But once it's gone what to rely upon?
Tangible is replaceable
With collectable references of time
But in the end
Whatever do we know?

To dust we go. Dust we must
When everything I know turns into dust
And everything we see loses its trust
Then all our life
Is what we can't see
I believe that's the only reality

There are some that will

There are some that will and some that won't,
And some who do, and some who don't.
And some who never can.
The will you have to practice?
It doesn't come that smooth.

The won't you have to fight against if you want to know the truth
The truth you have to leave behind.
The don't to have to kill.
And when you've managed all of this you'll say,
I do I will.

Let's all return to smaller days

Let's all return to smaller days, where we can work out smaller ways.
Put them altogether, and we have our bigger days, which are not so confusing.
Let's all return to smaller days of love and peace and hope and praise, and thanks for all the things we have.
Smaller days are easier to see, not so confusing, more consistency; smaller days in tiny ways help us to control our bigger days.
Bigger days become confusing—too much pain, crazy, abuse, wrong conclusions to create the illusion, put them into fusion, and you cannot move.
Smaller days create smaller ways or easier to see life has no pattern except you make and take your choice, and use your voice to express as loud as you can.
Why not if you can understand?

Wintertime is here

Wintertime is here.
Flowers are dying; people cry, the season's very near,
Gloves upon cold hands; cover up, it is clear.
As we gaze at lost years of happiness, sadness, and all its fears,
Time gone by, laughter and tears.

Wintertime is here; the leaves have gone and Disappeared into a maze,
A dancing haze of dazzling days.
But in the spring, the summer comes, and in the park are kids and mums,
And lovers taking time to see.

Wintertime is here; a cold wind that will not disappear.
Moving to a brand-new year.
No reflections on the past,
But connections in the future that will last.

Where was I before
I said I was

Where was I before I said I was it because someone said I was
And I became I was but what was that before I said I was
Was it because someone said I was
Where was I before I said I was
Was it because someone said I was
And then someone said you are
And I became you are who was I why you are
And then I started to find a place in my brain
To remain and starting to function as a you are
And everywhere I went I was here you are
And I gradually got better at being you are and I forgot who I was
before I said I was

Where was I before I said I was
Was it because someone said I was
And then they said you are and finally this is
And I was on the road to becoming not and I was not a you are
But this is this is what what this is this because it is this why is it this
Because it is this so all my understanding is a mixture of where was I
why and you are
And finally is you can't miss this is is this is this is this is
And finally you become a person with thousands of identities of other
people.
Not you at all.
Were you ever?
What about before someone said I was where was I before I said I was
was it because someone said I was

Welcome Home

I move silently through your life
Kicking up the leaves as I walk by
Uprooting what is hidden to be revealed
I cause a stirring in your inner being

I talk of change and challenge your ideals
Of how life should be and to be present
Got to keep moving, no time to keep still
Need to shed the skins of yesterday's tears

I support you with love as you move cautiously forward
Stepping into the swirling winds of the unknown
Such subtle vibrations keep pushing and pushing
Pushing you in the direction of home

Stay anchored and bravely lead your ship
As you arrive at the shores of freedom and rebirth
You fall into the arms of your loving self
Warmed by the flickering amber fire of the cauldron

I silently slip away but will remain by your side
And as you take the baton and shine your light
You will feel me in the sun, winds and the rains
Beckoning you forwards to share your knowledge and insights

**Written by Susan Evans / North London Hospice Compassionate
Neighbour**

Notes and Reflections

Notes and Reflections

Notes and Reflections

Printed and bound by CPI Group (UK) Ltd, Croydon, CR0 4YY